HOW TO DRAW DYNAMIC JAPANESE ANIME CHARACTERS ACTIVITY BOOK

JUPITER KIDS

JUPITER KIDS
CHILDREN'S & KIDS FICTION

INSTRUCTIONS FOR DRAWING:

THIS HOW-TO DRAWING BOOK CONSISTS OF IMAGES THAT ARE PLACED ON GRIDS. THERE IS A DRAWING BOX LOCATED AT THE LOWER PART OF THE PAGE AND THAT WILL SERVE AS YOUR PRACTICE SPACE. TO COPY THE IMAGE, DRAW PARTS OF THE IMAGE PER GRID AND PUT THEM ON THE BIGGER GRIDS. SOUNDS DIFFICULT? NOT REALLY. TRY IT FIRST!

IT'S OKAY IF YOU DON'T COPY THE IMAGE PERFECTLY. AFTER ALL, DRAWING IS ABOUT THE EXPRESSION OF YOUR PERCEPTION AS WELL AS YOUR HAND STRENGTH AND CONTROL.

WHEN YOU'VE COPIED THE IMAGE, GO AND AHEAD AND COLOR IT NEXT! WE'RE EXCITED TO SEE WHAT YOU CAN DO!

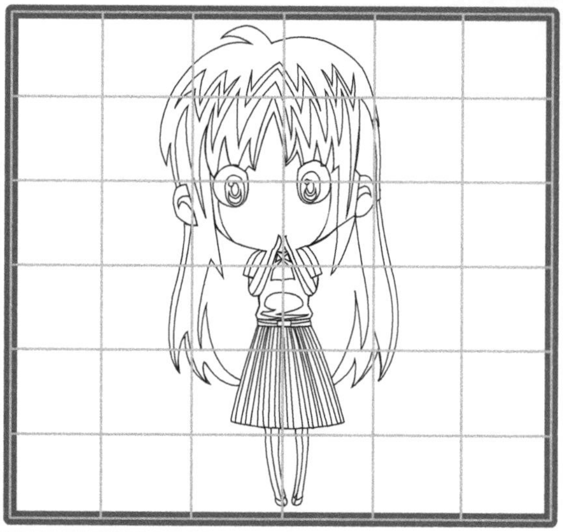

DRAW THE IMAGE

DRAW
THE IMAGE

DRAW
THE IMAGE

This is a Bleed Through Page If You Are Using a Coloring Marker or Pen!

DRAW THE IMAGE

DRAW THE IMAGE

DRAW
THE IMAGE

DRAW THE IMAGE

DRAW
THE
IMAGE

DRAW THE IMAGE

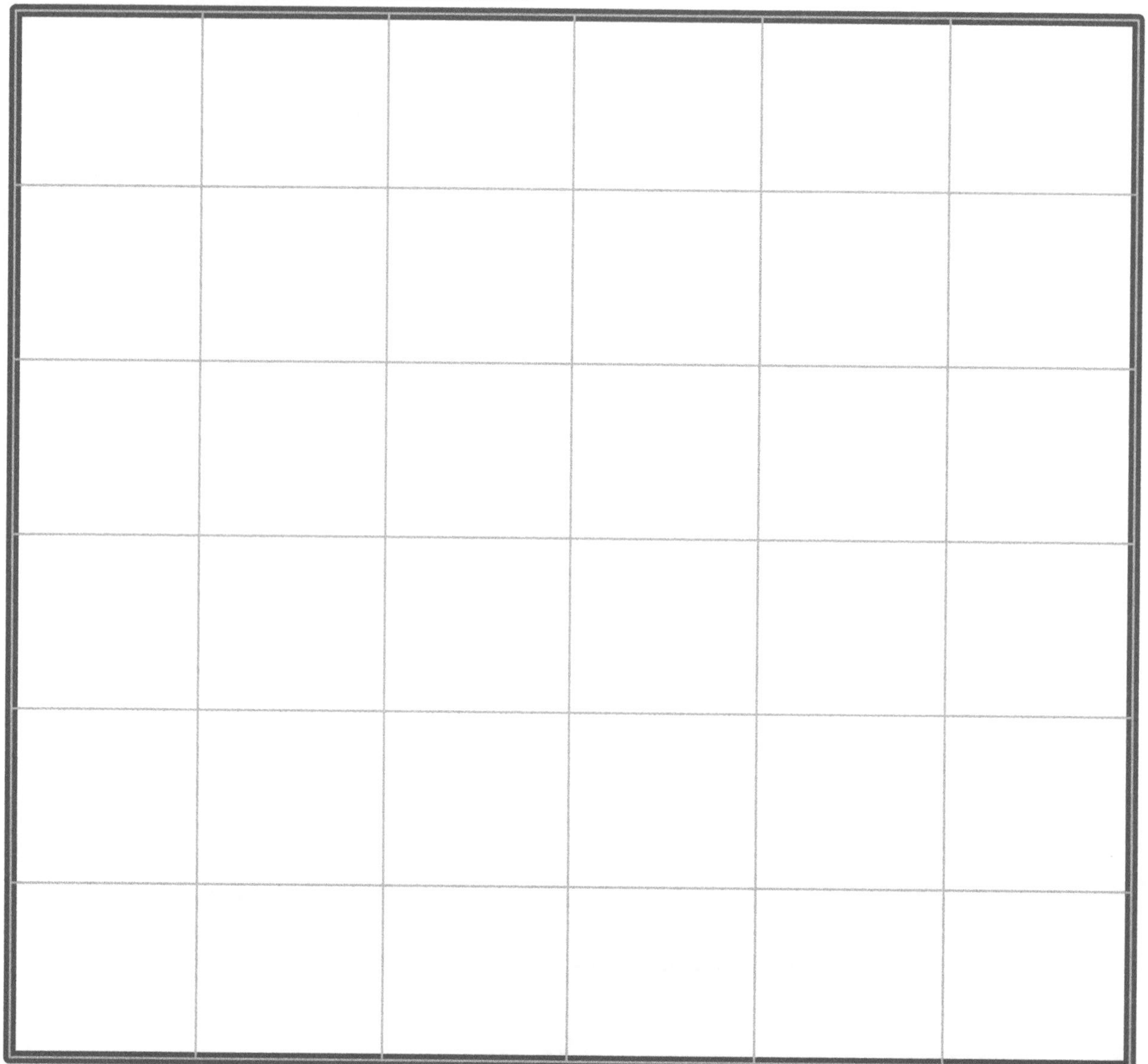

DRAW
THE
IMAGE

DRAW
THE
IMAGE

DRAW THE IMAGE

DRAW THE IMAGE

DRAW THE IMAGE

DRAW THE IMAGE

DRAW THE IMAGE

DRAW THE IMAGE

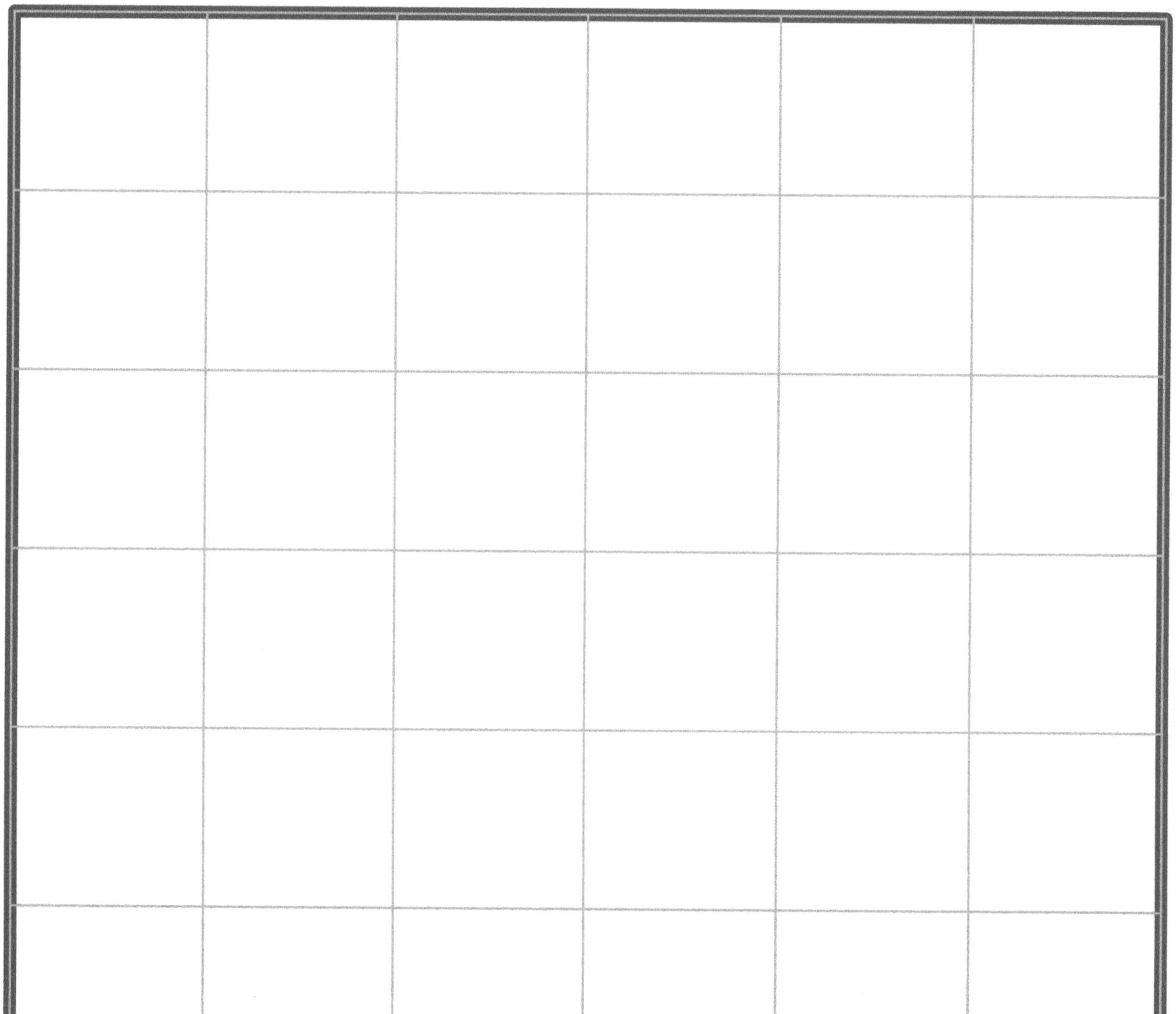

DRAW
THE IMAGE

DRAW THE IMAGE

This is a Bleed Through Page If You Are Using a Coloring Marker or Pen!

Find Other Great Titles By searching for Jupiter Kids on Your Favorite Book Retailer

Amazon.Com | Barnes & Noble (BN.Com) | Books A Million (BAM.Com)

JUPITER KIDS
CHILDREN'S & KIDS FICTION

DRAW THE IMAGE

DRAW THE IMAGE

DRAW
THE IMAGE

DRAW THE IMAGE

DRAW THE IMAGE

DRAW THE IMAGE

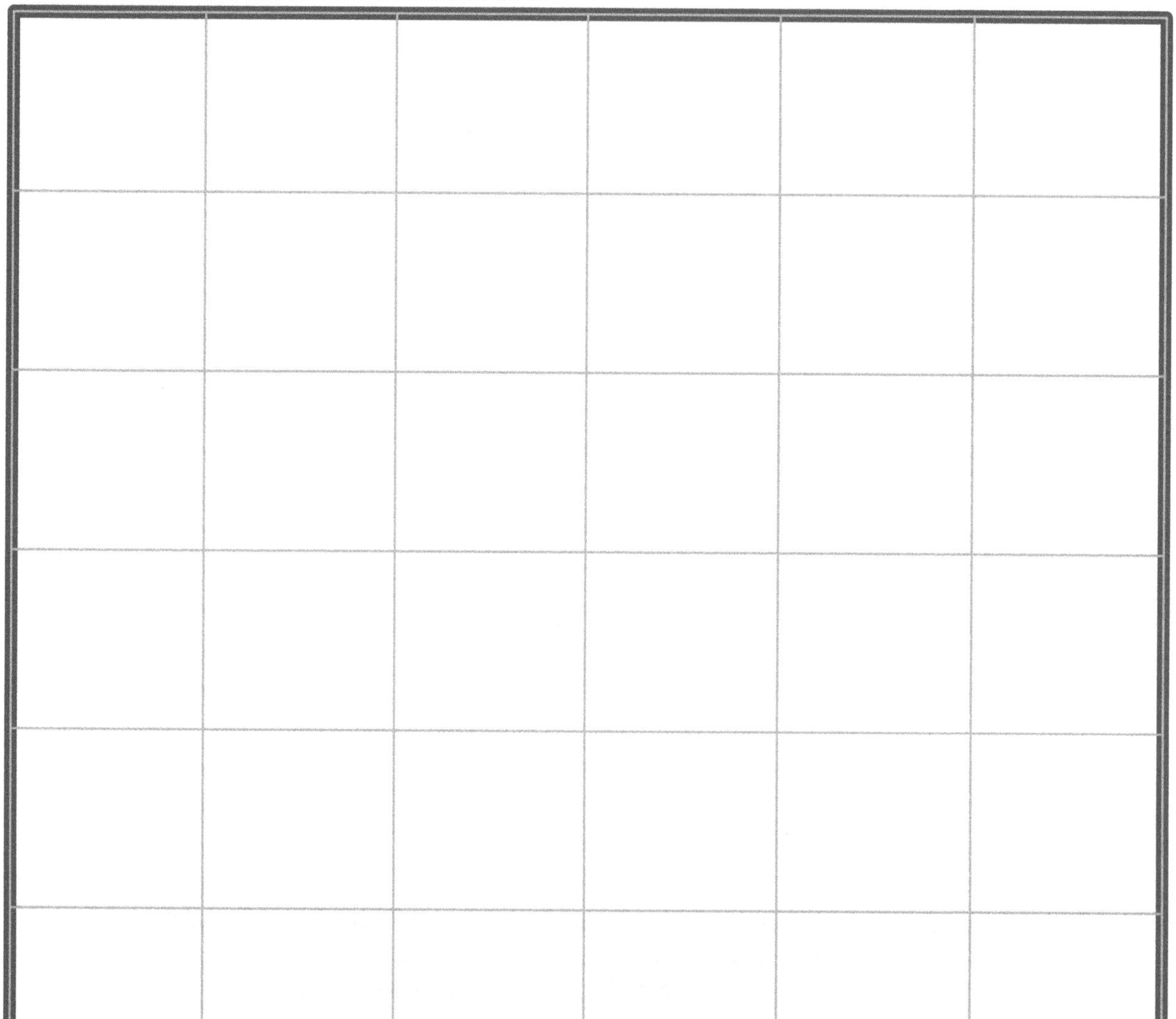

DRAW THE IMAGE

DRAW THE IMAGE

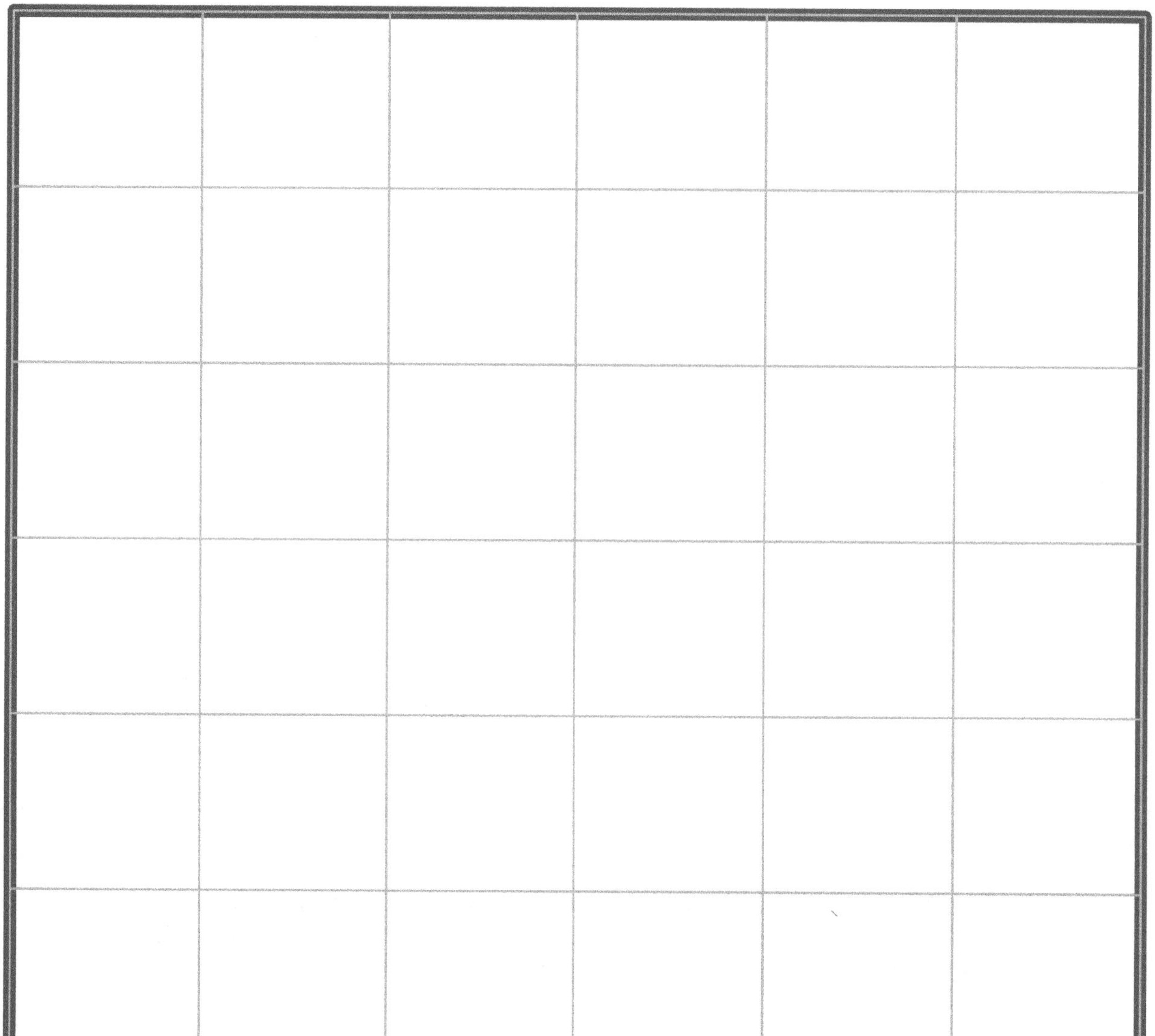

DRAW THE IMAGE

DRAW THE IMAGE

DRAW THE IMAGE

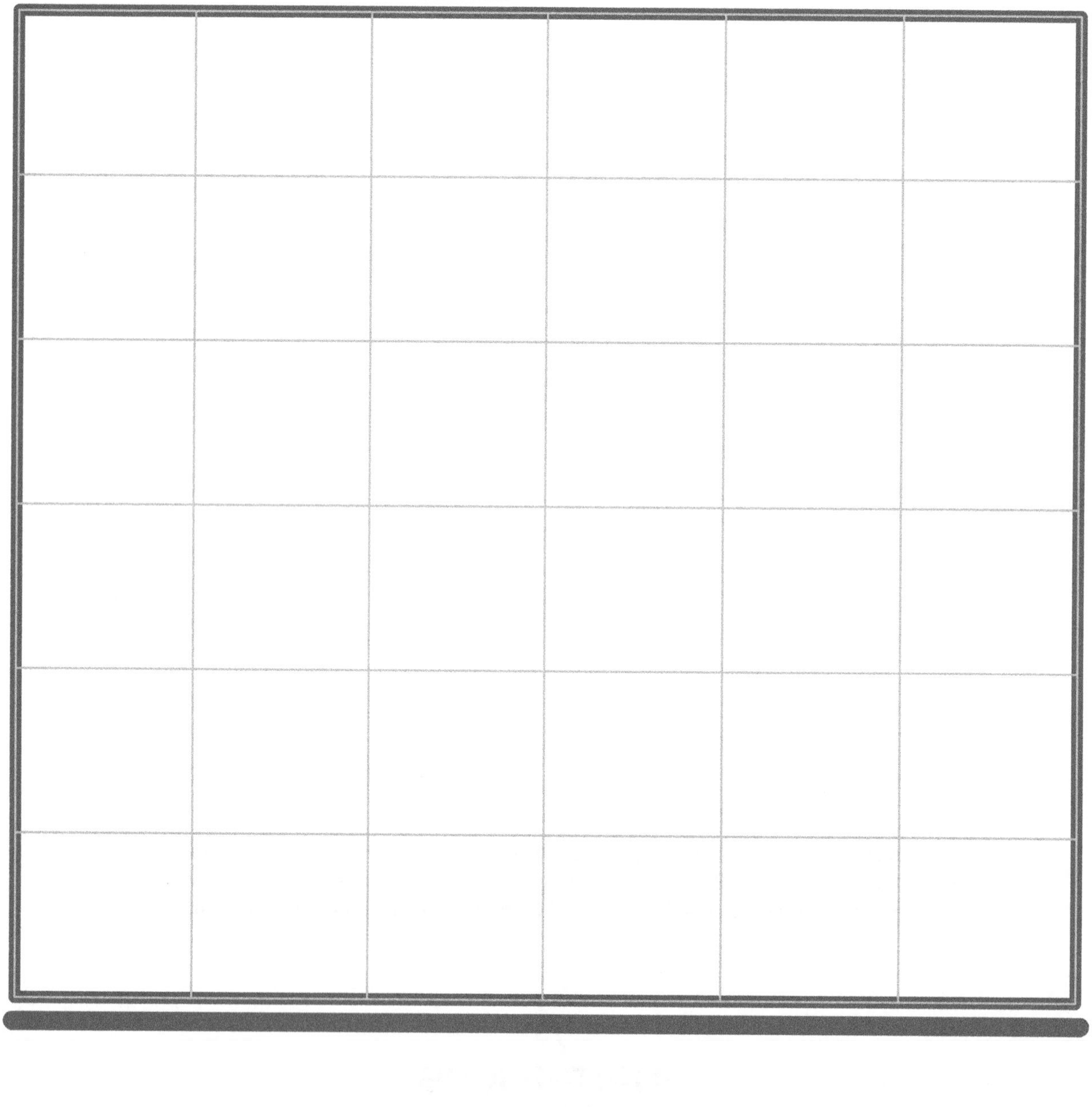

DRAW
THE IMAGE

DRAW
THE IMAGE

DRAW

THE IMAGE

DRAW THE IMAGE

DRAW THE IMAGE

DRAW
THE
IMAGE

DRAW THE IMAGE

DRAW
THE IMAGE

DRAW THE IMAGE

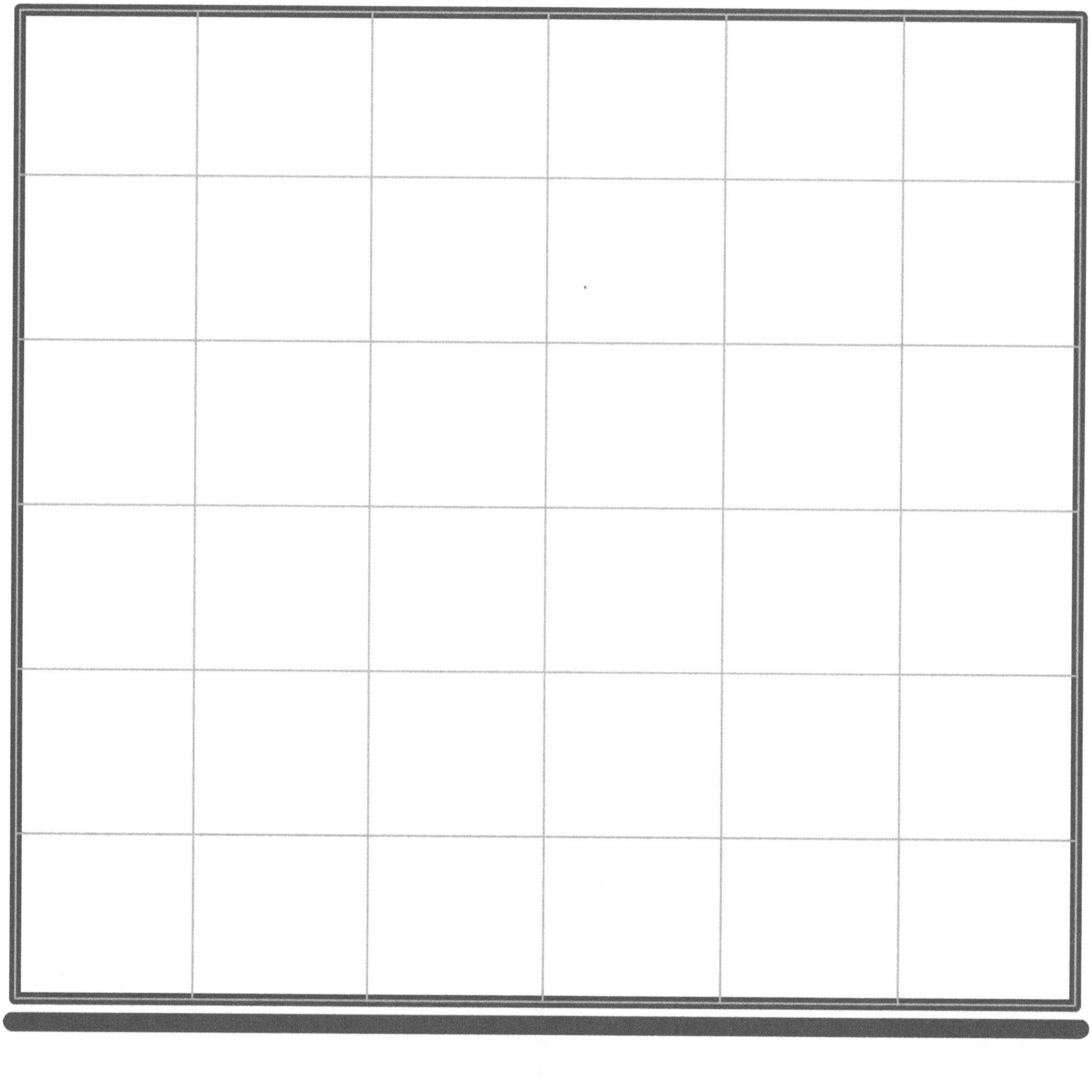

DRAW
THE IMAGE

DRAW
THE IMAGE

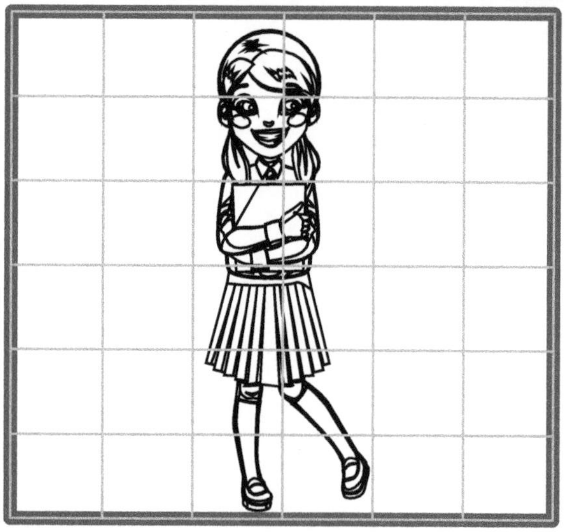

DRAW
THE
IMAGE

DRAW THE IMAGE

DRAW THE IMAGE

DRAW
THE IMAGE

DRAW THE IMAGE

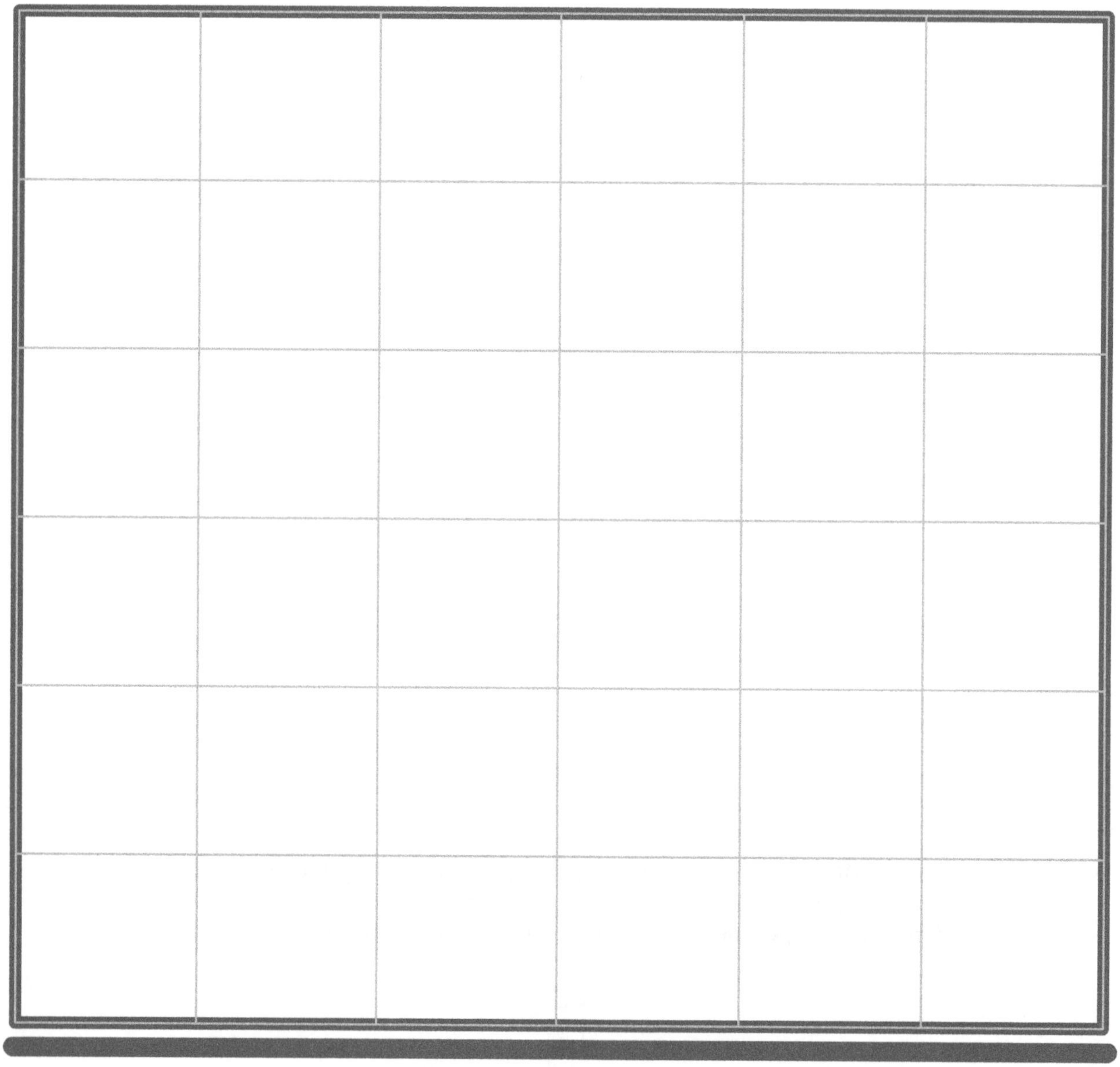

DRAW THE IMAGE

DRAW THE IMAGE

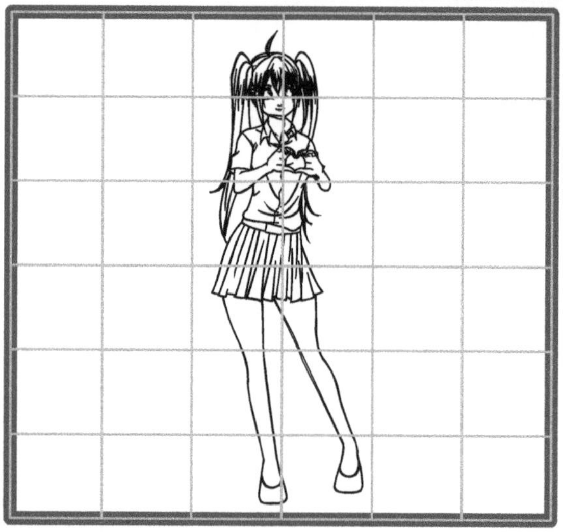

DRAW THE IMAGE

DRAW THE IMAGE

DRAW
THE IMAGE

Lightning Source UK Ltd.
Milton Keynes UK
UKHW050625051222
413416UK00014B/672

9 781683 269427